SOUTH AMERICA

SOUTH AMERICA

HANS MANN

241 PICTURES IN PHOTOGRAVURE, 5 IN COLOUR
INTRODUCTORY ESSAY, 21 MAPS
NOTES ON THE PLATES

A STUDIO PUBLICATION
THOMAS Y. CROWELL COMPANY
NEW YORK

ALL RIGHTS RESERVED 1957

PRINTED IN GREAT BRITAIN: COLOUR AND MONOCHROME GRAVURE

BY CLARKE AND SHERWELL LIMITED, NORTHAMPTON

LETTERPRESS BY JARROLD AND SONS LIMITED, NORWICH

SOUTH AMERICA

The belief that America was first discovered by Christopher Columbus is
based upon a misconception. Docu-
ments found in the Vatican towards
the close of the last century prove that
the Vikings reached Labrador in
about the year 1000, leaving again
after some 20 years.

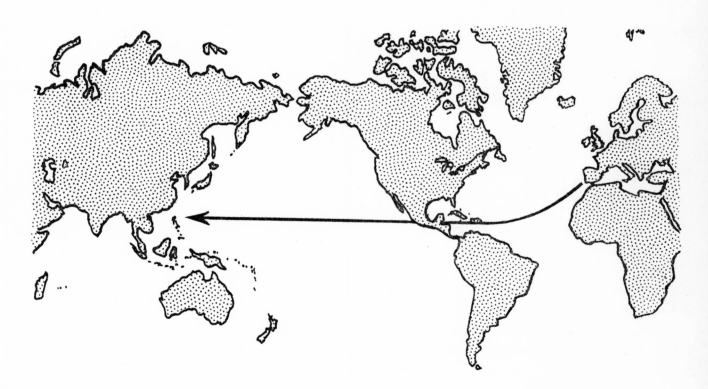

Columbus himself was under a
misapprehension, in that he believed
that he had found the route to the
Indies. He was unaware that he had
discovered—or, rather, re-discovered
—a vast new continent.

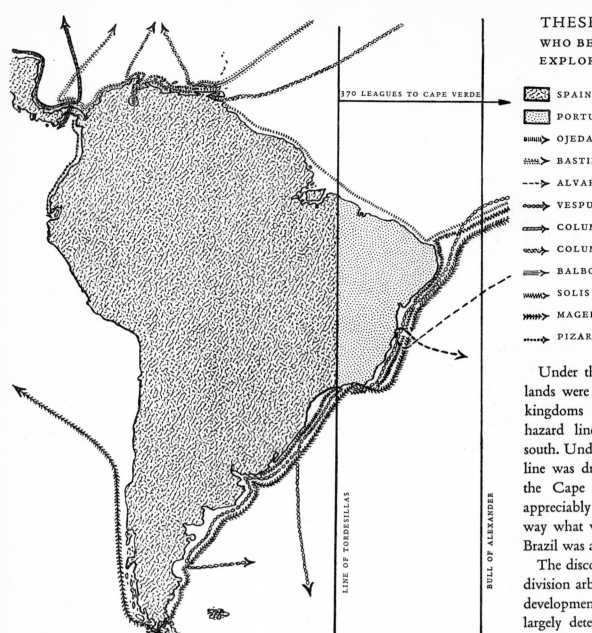

THESE WERE THE MEN
WHO BETWEEN 1499 AND 1526
EXPLORED THE COASTLINE

- SPAIN
- PORTUGAL
- OJEDA-VESPUCCIO 1499
- BASTIDAS-JUAN DE LA CASA 1500
- ALVAREZ GABRAL 1500
- VESPUCCIO 1502
- COLUMBUS 1504
- COLUMBUS THIRD VOYAGE
- BALBOA 1513
- SOLIS 1515
- MAGELLAN 1519-1521
- PIZARRO 1524-1526

370 LEAGUES TO CAPE VERDE

LINE OF TORDESILLAS

BULL OF ALEXANDER

Under the first, still undiscovered lands were divided between the two kingdoms by a more or less haphazard line drawn from north to south. Under the second, the dividing line was drawn 370 leagues west of the Cape Verde Islands; that is, appreciably farther westward. In this way what was later to be known as Brazil was allocated to Portugal.

The discovery was fortuitous and the division arbitrary; yet the subsequent development of South America was largely determined by the Treaty of Tordesillas.

Adverse winds obliged Columbus, when returning to Spain from his first voyage in 1492, to enter a Portuguese port. Through this, King John II of Portugal became aware of the discovery—made in the name of the Catholic Monarchs. This started a dispute between Spain and Portugal for possession of the newly found lands.

With a view to settling this bitter dispute, the highest authority of the day, Pope Alexander VI, was appealed to. He thereupon issued the famous Bull of May 4, 1493, known as the Partition of the World. This was superseded, a year later, by the Treaty of Tordesillas.

EARLY CARTOGRAPHERS

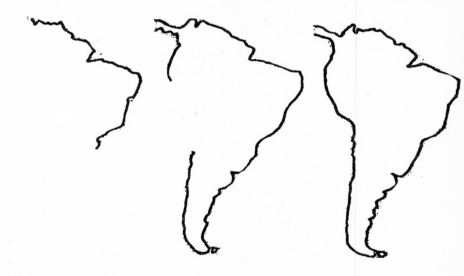

THE NAME "AMERICA" APPEARS FOR THE FIRST TIME IN THE MAP OF WALDSEEMUELLER (1507)

THIS IS HOW RIBERO SAW SOUTH AMERICA (1529)

IT WAS MERCATOR WHO FIRST COMPLETED THE OUTLINE (1569)

The conquest of America was carried through by men whose achievements and endurance far exceeded anything modern man is able to comprehend. Those who deplore that in the course of their search for new lands the conquistadors destroyed lives, cultures and cities, must remember the times in which these men lived. They and the countries they represented were prepared to go to any lengths in pursuing two basic aims: the acquisition of riches and the spreading of the Faith.

To attain these objectives they were ready to face fearful odds: they penetrated virgin forests, crossed fast-flowing rivers often many miles wide, traversed enormously high mountain ranges and navigated uncharted seas in crude vessels which they had to build themselves on inhospitable shores. Lacking roads and vehicles and far from their bases, they needed great courage and tenacity for such undertakings.

Their numbers progressively reduced by sickness, hardship and hostile inhabitants, these pioneers covered thousands of miles to win new empires for their sovereign lieges. In carrying out this task, a decisive factor was the horse.

LINE OF TORDESILLAS

▨	CHIBCHA EMPIRE
▤	INCA EMPIRE
▦	SAVAGE TRIBES
••••▶	ROUTES OF PENETRATION

THESE WERE THE MEN

WHO BETWEEN 1525 AND 1580 EXPLORED AND CONQUERED THE CONTINENT
AND FOUNDED THE FIRST COMMUNITIES OF WHITE MEN

SPANISH 1525 Rodrigo de Bastidas founds Santa Marta
1527 Sebastian Cabot founds Sancti Spiritus
1527 to 1541 Francisco Pizarro explores and conquers Peru
1532 to 1537 Diego de Almagro explores and conquers Bolivia
1534 Pedro de Alvarado founds Quito
1537 Domingo Martinez de Irala founds Asuncion
1538 Gonzalo Pizarro reaches Charcas and north of Chile
1539 Gimenez de Quesada founds Bogota
1541 Pedro de Valdivia founds Santiago de Chile
1542 Orellana descends the Napo and Amazon to the Atlantic
1567 Diego de Losada founds Caracas
1573 to 1580 Juan de Garay founds Santa Fé and Buenos Aires

PORTUGUESE 1532 Martin Alfonso de Souza founds San Vicente
1554 Foundation of São Paulo
1565 Mem de Sá founds Rio de Janeiro

South America can be divided into three main regions:

A MOUNTAINOUS WESTERN REGION

formed by high cordilleras and plateaus, geologically speaking of recent origin, which constitute a lofty backbone running parallel and comparatively close to the Pacific coast.

A FLAT CENTRAL REGION

formed by a succession of plains of sedimentary provenance, with smooth undulations and traversed by important networks of rivers.

Geological and palaeontological studies have established that far back in prehistory South America was an integral part of 'Gondwanaland', a vast continent which also comprised Africa, India, Australasia and the Antarctic. Subsequently, great upheavals caused the Atlantic and Indian Oceans to form, isolating South America except for its narrow link with the northern continent, and giving it its present outline.

All but the northernmost part of South America lies in the Southern Hemisphere, the bulk of it between the Equator and the Tropic of Capricorn.

AN EASTERN PLATEAU REGION

consisting of ancient rock formations covered by sedimentary layers and more recent volcanic outcrops. In this region erosion is very marked.

The conquest and opening up of the New World was no easy task. Geographically and topographically it presented great difficulties to the men from Europe. They had to face physical hardship on account of the terrain and climatic contrasts, and the distances exceeded anything they had hitherto known.

The SPANIARDS found EMPIRES and GOLD

on penetrating the interior of South America from the Antilles, where they had already established bases. The indigenous peoples they encountered had reached a high level of civilization and culture, and they clearly had large sources of gold.

Once the native chiefs had been subdued, the people, accustomed to obey, submitted to their new masters.

In less than half a century the Spaniards extended their dominion to the Pacific coast, the high plateau lands and the fertile valleys of the Cordillera over a distance of 4,800 kilometres.

4

What they may have first seen were dwellings on poles standing in the water. These gave its name to Venezuela—'Little Venice'.

5

6

Jungles and marshes constituted insurmountable obstacles.

7

8

Gold ornaments worn by the natives provoked a frenzied search for the metal and its source.

9

The newcomers were much harried by the natives, who impede the progress of the white man to this day

10

BALBOA discovers the Pacific Ocean in 1513

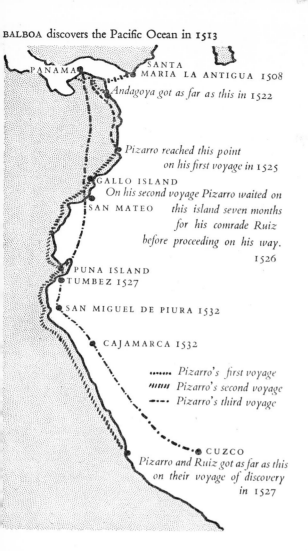

PANAMA

SANTA
MARIA LA ANTIGUA 1508
Andagoya got as far as this in 1522

Pizarro reached this point
on his first voyage in 1525
GALLO ISLAND
On his second voyage Pizarro waited on
SAN MATEO   *this island seven months*
for his comrade Ruiz
before proceeding on his way.
1526

PUNA ISLAND
TUMBEZ 1527

SAN MIGUEL DE PIURA 1532

CAJAMARCA 1532

······ *Pizarro's first voyage*
ııııı *Pizarro's second voyage*
–··–· *Pizarro's third voyage*

CUZCO
Pizarro and Ruiz got as far as this
on their voyage of discovery
in 1527

11

Once the Pacific Ocean had been discovered, a less hazardous route presented itself. Navigating southwards, the Spaniards explored the west coast of the continent.

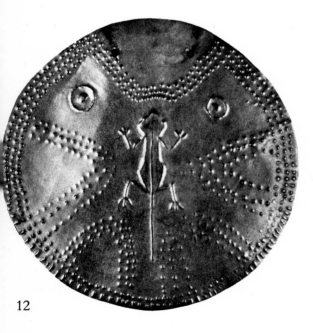

12   13

Exquisite works of art of strange designs bore witness to the high degree of evolution attained by the indigenous peoples of these regions. Fresh discoveries of gold enhanced the greed of the conquistadors.

14

16

the ruins of Chan Chan,

Farther south still, in Peru, they came upon wonders that far exceeded their wildest dreams. And what they saw impresses us even today:

ruined Paramonga,

15

17

the reliefs of Chan Chan,

19

innumerable specimens of artistic pottery.

the columns of Sechin,

18

20

21

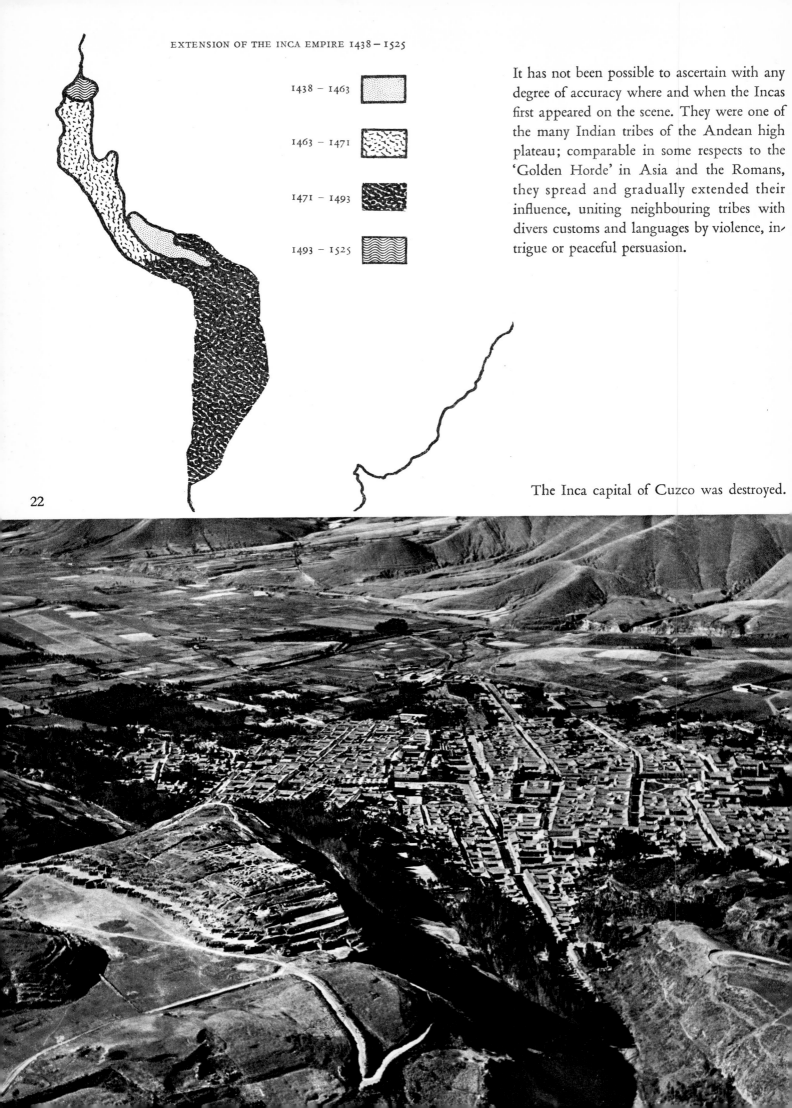

EXTENSION OF THE INCA EMPIRE 1438 – 1525

1438 – 1463	
1463 – 1471	
1471 – 1493	
1493 – 1525	

It has not been possible to ascertain with any degree of accuracy where and when the Incas first appeared on the scene. They were one of the many Indian tribes of the Andean high plateau; comparable in some respects to the 'Golden Horde' in Asia and the Romans, they spread and gradually extended their influence, uniting neighbouring tribes with divers customs and languages by violence, intrigue or peaceful persuasion.

The Inca capital of Cuzco was destroyed.

22

In the course of several centuries the Incas established an enormous empire, extending from the south of present-day Colombia to the borders of Argentina and Chile, upon which they imposed their rule.

Nevertheless, the Spaniards, who started their invasion from San Miguel de Piura, overran most of the Inca territory.

23

But portions of the buildings remain to this day.

24

25

The Incas built a vast network of roads linking all parts of their empire, one of which the Spaniards were to use in order to penetrate into the valleys of the Cordillera.

This area was tree-less at the time; trees were only introduced during the colonization.

The llamas, domesticated many centuries earlier, provided the natives with meat, wool, means of transportation and fertilizer —thus contributing materially to the prosperity of the Inca empire. The communities of Indians grew corn, beans, different varieties of potato, etc., delivering all their produce to the State, which in turn took charge of distribution and storage. An elaborate system of irrigation enabled the land to be intensively cultivated.

[20]

29

The Incas knew how to construct cities—such as Machu Picchu—on sites that remained hidden until quite recently.

30

Their walls were built to last
and were used as foundations
by the colonizers.

31

The PORTUGUESE *found* SAVAGES *and* TIMBER

but little else, on exploring the portion of the continent assigned to them by the Treaty of Tordesillas. In place of riches they had to be content with logs of 'lignum brasile', a wood already known in Europe. After it the vast land of Brazil was named.

The humid, unhealthy jungles of the north, through which flows the Amazon, were unpropitious for colonization.

Nor were conditions much more favourable along the central stretches of the Atlantic coast.

The Portuguese therefore settled farther south, in the protected bays around what is now the port of Santos.

Savages and warrior tribes prevented the newcomers from penetrating into the interior.

32

33

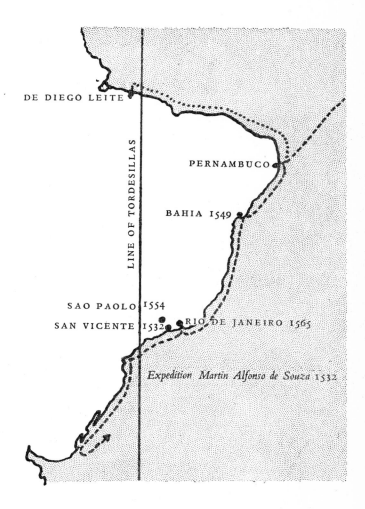

Since they had found no gold, interest at home in their exploits waned; it was now concentrated upon the routes to the East Indies already established around the Cape of Good Hope.

But the news that a Spanish expedition under Cabot had sailed up the River Plate, not far from Portuguese territory, impelled the Portuguese Crown to occupy these lands. It was not until 1530, when the Spaniards were actively engaged in their conquest of the Inca empire, that the Portuguese began to establish themselves in places easy of access and readily defensible.

These places they quickly colonized, planting sugar cane brought from the Cape Verde Islands.

The interior was not penetrated until after intermarriage had brought into being a mestizo population.

The Indians of the jungle led a very primitive existence, living on wild game and fish.

35

37

38

39

Here were no organized communities or developed cultures comparable with those the Spaniards met with.

40

41

42

43

A humanitarian and civilizing influence

was exercised by the Catholic priests, who did much to check the worst excesses of the conquerors. At first it was the Franciscans, Dominicans and Fathers of Mercy; but the chief rôle was played by the Jesuits, especially in the Indian missions of Paraguay, the River Plate area and other Spanish-held territories.

The Jesuits started their work at the beginning of the seventeenth century in Misiones, Corvientes, Paraguay and parts of the Brazilian states of Santa Catalina and Rio Grande. They founded 33 missions run on the basis of compulsory work for all able-bodied men, division of benefit amongst the entire community and realisation of surpluses. Except for an insignificant tribute, no taxes were payable.

To them were due the first plantations of yerba mate, tobacco, cotton, sugar cane, vines, fruit trees; the clearing of jungles and forests, and livestock breeding. But it was on a cultural plane that their work attained its greatest importance.

They taught the Indians how to develop industries and at the same time converted them to the Christian faith, inculcating in them the habits of work, discipline and instruction. They compiled books in rudimentary printing-shops which they themselves constructed, and taught painting, sculpture, architecture and music. In their eagerness to protect the Indians against the unscrupulous conquerors, they prohibited the residence of Whites in the missions.

In 1767, Charles III of Spain ordered the expulsion of the Jesuits from Spain and the colonies, fearing the power which their civilizing work had brought for them. As a result, the missions rapidly deteriorated and many of the Indians returned to their primitive savage life.

44

45

48

46

47

49

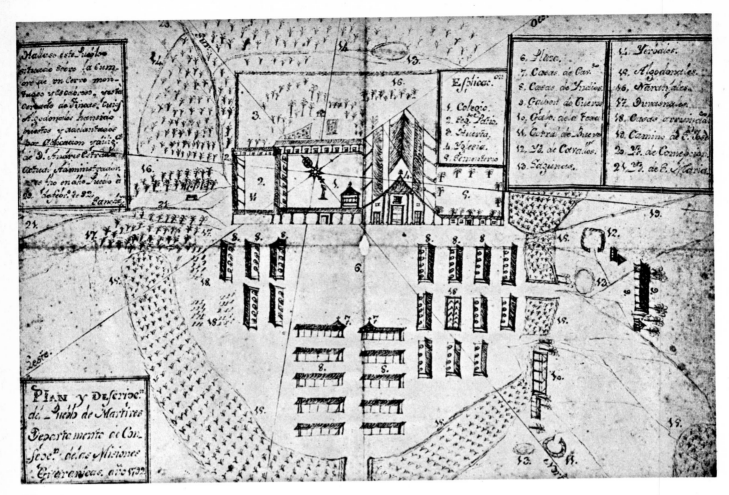

50

51

52

COLOUR PLATE II
HARVESTING IN THE HIGHLANDS OF ECUADOR

In Spain,

after the union of Castile and Aragon through the marriage of the Catholic Monarchs, the monarchy asserted its political and religious power over the nation. The King was the absolute power, and in the name of the King the conquest was carried out by the 'adelantados'. Certain gentlemen received this title who, in exchange for totally or partially equipping the expedition, had the right to 'conquer, govern and exploit' American lands, and the obligation to impose the royal authority, found cities, convert the natives and hand over to the King a part of their gains.

Unlike the Portuguese captains on whom the land was bestowed as hereditary property, the 'adelantados' were given possession of it 'for the span of their life' and sometimes also of that of their successor. But the King was the sole owner of the colonies and master of its inhabitants, patron of the churches that had been founded and the only individual with the right to appoint and dismiss officials.

The authorities appointed by the King to govern the colonies changed as time went on: the 'adelantados' were succeeded by governors—officials with salaries—and these by the captains. Finally, the viceroyalties and general captaincies were created.

The constant interference by the King in the conquest and exploitation of the colonies—governed by a set of laws also drawn up under royal authority—made impossible even those rudimentary autonomies which, in the case of the Portuguese, so much contributed to fostering the ideas of 'nation' and 'fatherland'.

In regard to violence and cruelty, the Spanish conquerors did not resort to them in greater measure than other countries. Indeed, the conquest was endowed with a high humanitarian and civilizing spirit. This is proved by the 'Laws of the Indies', a document of profound ethical and religious feeling designed to protect the souls, life and well-being of the American Indians.

Under these laws they had to be educated and converted to Catholicism; to deprive them of their freedom or possessions was forbidden; no form of servitude could be imposed on them nor were they allowed to be sold or exchanged by the conquerors. They precisely regulated the services rendered by the natives and established the maximum daily hours of work, obligatory remuneration and other rights, to a degree that the social legislation of other countries only attained centuries later. Unfortunately, they were drawn up without an exact knowledge of the localities where they had to be applied and of the people to be protected, with the result that they were violated many times even by those responsible for their enforcement.

The royal prerogatives also weighed on the trade of the colonies. Excessive interference on the part of the authorities and a rigorous control impeded a progressive interchange of goods; this was further handicapped by a total protectionism: the subject territories could only trade with Spain.

This permanent subordination to the King, the clearly commercial nature of the enterprise and the absence of stabilizing activities—such as agriculture—discouraged permanent Spanish settlers. What predominated was the exploitation of those things that were readily negotiable, metals in particular, and towards the end of the seventeenth century, livestock and timber. At the beginning, the sole aim of agriculture was to supply local needs, without any thought of export.

All the measures which restricted freedom, though they were inspired by the aim to assure Spanish dominion over the colonial empire, finally had a contrary effect, because they fostered resentment which later took the form of a rebellion against Spain.

Important factors prompting the struggle for independence towards the end of the eighteenth century were the liberal ideals spread by the European philosophers and American societies and lodges, the Independence of the United States and the French Revolution. The pioneers of the movement—Miranda in Venezuela and Pueyrredon in the River Plate—tried to attain independence with the help of Great Britain, at war at the time against Spain and France. The English Government promised help in exchange for commercial concessions.

The beginning of the revolution in Spanish America coincided with the Napoleonic invasion of the Peninsula which resulted in the renunciation of the Spanish throne by King Ferdinand VII and the flight of the Portuguese monarch to Brazil. The first indication of this revolution was the establishment of 'Government Juntas' at various points in the continent, which alleged that they administered the colonies 'in the name of the King'. They were composed for the most part of cultured creoles, who were determined to obtain an ultimate independence.

Their activities did not lead to a concerted plan of action, however; nor did they envisage a united nation bound by common ties.

When Ferdinand VII was restored to his throne in 1814, he immediately attempted to reincorporate the American colonies and thus started the wars of Independence whose two outstanding figures were Bolivar in the north and San Martin in the south. Ayachucho (1824), the last battle of this struggle, put an end to Spanish domination in America.

Thus, the rupture with Spain was brought about with great violence and bloodshed. Furthermore, the lack of spiritual cohesion of the Hispanic block, the diverse origin of its native populations and its immense size, prevented federation. The only link the lands have in common is the Spanish language; geographical and political unity, such as the Portuguese territories know, was never achieved.

COLOUR PLATE III

DEVIL MASK AT COPACABANA

the internal situation was very similar to that in Spain where royal absolutism was concerned, but the administration of the American colonies was not so centralized. To start with, the colonies did not belong to the King, but to the nation.

Portugal already had colonial experience, and on the strength of this decided to divide its American possessions into 'captaincies'. This name it gave to territories made over by the King—as an inalienable, indivisible and hereditary possession—to a 'captain'. A part of these lands remained the personal property of the 'captain', the remainder was leased to Christian colonizers who had to undertake to give the Crown a sixth part of their profits. Moreover, the Portuguese Government reserved for itself the commercial monopoly on Brazilian timber, the fifth part of all precious metals extracted and, later, all diamonds over twenty carats.

Thus, the Portuguese colonies had the advantage over the Spanish in that there was less interference from the Crown, and although we may scarcely talk about 'autonomy', in time this régime favoured the formation of a 'national' spirit. It is also worth mentioning that the Inquisition was never introduced into the Portuguese colonies.

With only two exceptions, the captaincies did not prosper, however; a situation that was further aggravated by piratical attacks from the sea and from the hinterland by the Indians. To co-ordinate assistance and protection, the King of Portugal appointed a Governor-General to whom the captaincies were subordinated. The first of these officials was appointed in 1549 with headquarters in Bahia, which were maintained there until Rio was declared the capital (1763).

The Portuguese supported agriculture in their South American lands, which tended more towards co-operation than exploitation by mining. The large owners, of the feudal type, lived surrounded by employees and servants and formed powerful groups, capable of defending themselves against any invader. They proved this against the French, who attempted to occupy a part of Brazil, and against the Dutch, whom it took them longer to defeat.

The French invasion, apart from engendering a form of patriotism among the people, caused them to extend their zone of colonization to the mouth of the Amazon. The Dutch invasion had even more important consequences, because it provided the first proof that the 'national spirit' was a reality. This was in 1654, when Indians, Negroes and Whites united in the 'Pernambuco Rebellion' to defend something which they considered their own, though they received no help, and despite the fact that Lisbon had recognized the Dutch Government.

Between 1580 and 1640, Portugal was subject to Spain, and the boundary line established by the Treaty of Tordesillas was no longer in force.

From San Pablo, where a flourishing colony had already been established, the 'bandeiras' started to penetrate into the interior. They were thus dubbed because, carrying a flag as an emblem, groups of 50 to 500 'bandeirantes' went in search of slaves for their plantations. They had a further aim—to find 'the country of gold and precious stones' about which they had heard the Indians speak. They left the coastal region to advance towards the south, west and north, and while some of them took up cattle-raising others continued their march, opening the way to subsequent colonization of the interior.

When Portugal regained her independence, the Spaniards sought to re-establish the Tordesillas line, but it was too late: the 'bandeirantes' had extended the frontiers of the country almost to their present limits.

It was also the 'bandeirantes' who discovered gold and diamonds in the hinterland, and although the colony retained the dominant characteristics imparted by agriculture and forestry, this powerful inducement temporarily caused the current economic system to be modified.

Apart from creating wealth, the gold led indirectly to the first attempt to attain independence. The families enriched by the precious metals sent their sons to European universities, where they came into contact with the ideas spread by the Declaration of Independence of the United States. Inspired by those ideas, some of them engaged in a conspiracy on their return to Brazil, but it failed. Their leader, nick-named 'Tiradentes' because he was a dentist, was sent to the gallows.

The Napoleonic invasion of Portugal constituted the most important factor in arousing the Brazilian national conscience: the Regent, Prince John, fled with all his court to his colony, which thereby became an empire in itself. The country no longer had overseas links, and constituted a political and geographical unit.

Thirteen years later the sovereign returned to Lisbon with his court, leaving his son, Peter, as Regent of Brazil. But there was a popular outcry for independence; whereupon the Regent, interpreting the sentiment of the people, assumed the crown of the new independent empire as Peter I (1822). The Regency of 1831 and the accession of Peter II in 1840, merely delayed the advent of the Republic, which was definitely established in 1889.

The rupture with the metropolis was thus achieved without bloodshed, at a time when the people of the colony were already united in spirit.

The Guianas . . .

Shared between Spain and Portugal, the American territory aroused the covetousness of other Powers which attempted, on more than one occasion, to establish themselves there by force. For geographical reasons, the Atlantic coast was the one most exposed to attack. The invaders, foiled south of the Amazon, turned their attention to the region north of its mouth.

It was at the point where the central fringe of the jungle reaches the coast of the Atlantic, in the Guianas, that they succeeded in their aims: Great Britain, Holland and France were able to create colonies which at no time were exposed to the pressure of either the Portuguese or the Spanish colonizers.

This was possible, in the first place, because of the isolated situation of the plateau of the Guianas, difficult to reach by land but easy of access from the sea. In the second place, since the vastness of South America obliged the Spaniards and Portuguese to concentrate their colonizing efforts on the most valuable parts, the region of the Guianas was left defenceless, allowing the occupying Powers to take and keep possession of it.

They owe their existence today still as the only European colonies in South America to the fact that their geographical situation did not—during the period of colonization —allow a native nucleus to be formed which would serve as the rallying-point for a 'national consciousness' such as carried the Spanish and Portuguese colonies to ultimate independence.

'The Continent of the Next Century'

Several factors influenced the development of the South American countries when they began to shape their destinies during the first quarter of the nineteenth century. Of great importance was the fact that the natives who lived there prior to the colonization comprised very diverse elements; the type of people resulting from the miscegenation of immigrant Europeans and Indians largely depended upon the level of civilization to which the latter had previously attained. Subsequent influxes of immigrants, together with the topographical and climatic features of the regions in which they settled, also played their part.

In the Andean highland region there were various indigenous civilizations long before the discovery of the Americas, and even today the majority of Indians live in this region. They speak their original languages and their customs go back many centuries. The strong racial characteristics of these people have led, in many cases, to an indianizing of the Europeans. Four hundred years after the conquest, the Indian element still predominates in the half-castes of the entire Andean range. About half the people of Peru, Bolivia and Ecuador are of pure Indian stock. Through their attitude of passive resistance they have been responsible for retarding the development of these countries.

In the central plains and eastern plateaux there is a mixed population of another kind. The Indians of these regions had no strong political or cultural traditions and have been absorbed by the Europeans. The Mestizos who live here take an active part in the affairs of the State to which they belong. This is particularly evident in regions where a good climate has attracted large numbers of European immigrants.

In the coastal areas of North Brazil, the Guianas, Venezuela and Colombia, the supply of native labour for the plantations began to fail about the middle of the sixteenth century. Large numbers of African slaves were imported, who soon acclimatized themselves in surroundings very similar to those of their native land. White and black intermingled, and as a result the population very largely consists of mulattos; their African origin can be recognized in their folk music and their dances. The crossing of Africans and Indians in the interior of the country is of less consequence.

During the nineteenth century a new wave of European immigrants spread over the vast plateaux of South Brazil and also over the fertile plains of Uruguay, south Argentina and central and southern Chile. Important economic and cultural centres have sprung up where they settled. However, the colonizers and settlers of South America confined themselves in the main to the coastal regions of the continent, for the enormous distances, the difficulty of the terrain and the lack of communications prevented them from moving far inland. The new governments were centred in those cities which were formerly the seats of the viceroys. Sections of the far-flung population lived at great distances from the capital and horses were the only means by which the authority of the government could reach the outlying regions to enforce laws, or collect taxes. Horses were also the only means of transporting goods. Only those who have ridden through the Pampas or crossed the Andes can fully appreciate what effect the enormous distances and the difficulty of the terrain has had on the development of South America.

The infancy of the South American countries coincided with an era in which the rapid flow of new inventions upset the social structure even of nations that had long had an established government. Furthermore, the remoteness of South America from those countries that were able to absorb technological advances by gradual stages meant that such developments were invariably introduced there later and sporadically. This,

COLOUR PLATE V
DOCKERS PLAYING DOMINOES AT SANTOS

v

coupled with the rather negative character of the people, has frequently impeded the advancement of the South American countries.

The adoption of technical inventions in South America has depended largely on the density of the population and the capital available, and their progress into the interior of the continent on the distance to be covered and the terrain. The introduction of the railways was the first step, and as all the materials for them had to come from overseas, their construction was more difficult there than in those more technically advanced countries which were able to provide for themselves, and where the population was large enough to ensure a sufficient yield on the capital thus invested. In the course of time the railways made their way far inland, and today they link up the various South American States. Yet, over vast areas of the continent people continued to depend on horses until the introduction of the automobile which caused a tremendous revolution in their lives.

South Americans virtually jumped from horseback into cars, trucks and tractors. The horseman was overwhelmed by the suddenness and the extent of the change wrought by the advent of the internal combustion engine. He had respect for his horse but none for these new-fangled machines. He had bred and trained his own horse, understood it and knew that it respected him. But with the machine it was quite different; he was not present when it was designed, he had never seen the factory where it was made, and he did not understand the long chain of processes which went into its production. It was suddenly there before him, complete—a thing of metal with no soul.

Clearly such an attitude retards mechanization, and in many areas in the interior of South America men still prefer to use animals, for it is easier to replace an exhausted horse than a broken machine which they cannot mend.

The horsemen who live on the endless expanses of the Pampas and in the valleys of the Andes regard time in a different light from us. Minutes, hours or even days mean very little to men who live close to nature; hence their unpunctuality and procrastination. But of recent years these people have developed the faculty of improvisation, which is essential in most parts of South America. A threshing machine cannot stand idle in harvest time, until some spare part is obtained from perhaps a hundred miles away; its owner must discover how to put it in order with whatever material he may have at hand. A geologist prospecting for tin in the Andes must use his cooking pot for laboratory work, when his last crucible is broken.

The advancement of the South American countries was accelerated by the First, and even more by the Second World War. Increased quantities of raw materials were required and with the help of modern techniques they were obtained much more rapidly. Methods of transportation improved and road networks were extended. Wheat, metals and oil were produced in ever increasing quantities. What is more, the flow of essentials from overseas was twice interrupted, with the result that South Americans felt the need to become self-supporting; a period of rapid industrialization began.

Here again the effects of their past can be seen. It is virtually impossible for an entirely agricultural people to become industrial in one generation. It is obvious that they will lack the skill and the sense of responsibility of European craftsmen and workers, and that they will not realize the value of social legislation for which they have not had to fight. Yet when all the negative factors, which have prevented the progress of the South American countries, have been taken into consideration, it is really remarkable how much has been achieved in a few years.

Air-transport has undoubtedly done most for the development of these parts of the world. Anyone familiar with the great open spaces of South America will be able to appreciate its value. From Rio it used to take a month by boat to reach Manaos in the centre of the Amazon basin. Today an aircraft covers the 1700 miles in eight or nine hours. Until quite recently, Bolivia depended on Argentina for her meat supplies; now an airport has been established in the almost uninhabited region of Beni, and the cattle that roamed wild in the woods and steppes since the Spaniard left the land have been rounded up. The strains have been improved by crossing with imported cattle, and a refrigeration plant, for which equipment was brought in by plane, has been installed. Now most Bolivians are supplied with home-bred meat distributed by air. A journey that not long ago used to take over a month is accomplished nowadays in about an hour and a half.

Air travel has brought the people of the provinces much closer to the capital. News-papers are available on the day of issue in most towns. Doctors can quickly reach the most remote places to treat or inoculate those whom otherwise they could only have reached by boat or on horseback. In short, it is entirely thanks to aircraft that the South American countries are learning to know themselves and their neighbours. Cultural and commercial interchange increases daily. The planes cover huge tracts of sparsely populated country and regions whose natural resources are as yet unexploited.

If, then, the South American countries can find a formula which will enable them to work together closely and effectively, they will have a great part to play in the world. South America is, without doubt, 'the continent of the next century'.

1. Andes range, Aconcagua territory (Argentina and Chile).
2. Llanos (Colombia and Venezuela).
3. Mountain formations near Rio de Janeiro (Brazil).
4, 8, 12, 13. Gold ornaments from Colombia (Colombia).
5. Pile-dwellings at Maracaibo (Venezuela).
6. Primeval forest near Barauca Bermejo (Colombia).
7. Swamp-land near Arauca (Colombia).
9. Jibaro Indian from Ecuador (Ecuador).
10. Dwelling of the Motilones Indians in the primeval forests of Perija (Colombia).
11. Terra-cotta head from Esmeralda (Ecuador).
14, 19–21. Ceramic ware in the State Museum at Lima (Peru).
15. Ruined Paramonga (Peru).
16. Ruins of Chan Chan (Peru).
17. Detail of a relief in Chan Chan (Peru).
18. Upright stone on a ruined site near Sechin (Peru).
22. Cuzco.
23. Indian from Pisac (Peru).
24. Ruins from Inca times near Cuzco (Peru).
25. Inca road on the Island of the Sun, Lake Titicaca (Bolivia).
26. Valley in the Cordilleras near Cuzco (Peru).
27. Llama among the high plateaux of the Andes (Peru).
28. Terraces near Machu Picchu (Inca: Peru).
29. Machu Picchu (Inca: Peru).
30. Wall from Inca times, with superimposed houses built by the Spaniards (Cuzco: Peru).
31. Wall from Inca times (Cuzco: Peru).
32. Countryside near Victoria, Espiritu Santo State (Brazil).
33. Mangrove-swamp in the Amazon region (Brazil).
34. Palms by the coast near Bahia (Brazil).
35, 36. Indians from the Amazon region (Brazil).
37. Piece of pottery made by the Tupi Indians (Brazil).
38–41. Indians from the interior of Brazil (Brazil).
42–49, 51, 52. Among the ruins of the San Ignacio Mini Jesuit Mission (Argentina) and Objects from the times of the Jesuits.
50. Plan of the 'Martires' Jesuit Mission (Argentina).

BIBLIOGRAPHY

Anuario DIC, *Diccionario Enciclopédico de la Universidad de Chile.*

Biografía del Caribe, *Germán Arciniegas.*

Brasil, Pais del Futuro, *Stefan Zweig.*

Brasilian Culture, *F. D. Acevedo.*

Casa Grande a Senzala, *Gilberto Freyre.*

Chile o Una Loca Geografia, *Benjamin Subercaceaux.*

Costa, Sierra y Montaña, *Miró Quesada.*

Diccionario Enciclopédico de las Américas, *Editorial Futuro S.R.L. B. Aires.*

Doña Bárbara, *Rómulo Gallegos.*

El Perú Prehispánico, *Hans Horkheimer.*

Encyclopédie de L'Amérique Latine, *Presses Universitaires de France.*

Handbook of South American Indians, *Smithsonian Institution.*

Historia de América, *Luis Alberto Sánchez.*

Historia de la Cultura Antigua del Perú, *Luis Valcarcel.*

L'Amérique Latine entre en scène, *Tibor Mende.*

Nueva Historia de Bolivia, *Enrique Finot.*

Oxford Economic Atlas of the World, *Oxford University Press.*

Publications on Latin American Republics, *Pan American Union, Washington D.C.*

Südamerika, *Kurt Pahlen.*

The Awakening Valley, *John Collier and Anibal Buitrón.*

The South American Handbook 1955–1956, *Edited by Howell Davies.*

Une Civilization du Miel, *Juan Velar.*

NOTES ON THE PLATES

VENEZUELA

Area: 352,150 square miles
Population: 5,440,000

There are four main geographical regions:

1 The Venezuelan Andes
2 The Maracaibo Lowlands
3 The Orinoco Lowlands
4 The Guiana Plateau

Exports:
Oil, iron, gold, diamonds, coffee and cocoa

53 *Derricks of the Creole Petroleum Company at Maracaibo*

Lake Maracaibo lies between the two most northerly arms of the Andes. Until 1917 this hot and humid region was inhabited only by small farming communities, but the discovery of petroleum in that year began an era of rapid change and Venezuela is now the second greatest oil-producing country in the world.

54 *Pile-dwellings in Lake Maracaibo*

In some places pile-dwellings are still being built, precisely like those which led the Spanish conquistadors to name this country Venezuela—'Little Venice'.

55 *Indian women of the Guajiro tribe*

Indian women of the Guajiro tribe, gaily dressed and with painted faces, watch with apparent unconcern the bustling activity of the modern port of Maracaibo.

56 *Workshops of the Creole Petroleum Company at Maracaibo*

57 *Staff living-quarters and oil storage tanks of the Company at Lagunillas on the edge of Lake Maracaibo*

The workshops and storage tanks of the Creole Petroleum Company cover many square miles, and a forest of oil derricks stretches far out into the lake. Nowadays about ninety per cent of Venezuela's national revenue comes from oil.

58 *A classroom in a school of the Creole Petroleum Company at Indivana on Lake Maracaibo*

59 *Children in front of a stall at Indivana on Lake Maracaibo*

60 *A worker of the Creole Petroleum Company*

The development of the oil region has been accelerated by the flow of capital and the very high level of employment, resulting in the highest standard of living on the entire continent. Officials and workers live in comfortable houses, well adapted to the climate; schools, hospitals, shops and recreation centres are multiplying rapidly.

61 *An unfinished road in Caracas*

62 *Colonial houses in the centre of Caracas*

63 *A street in a suburb of Caracas*

The capital, Caracas, lies in a fertile valley of the Andes, about 3100 feet above sea-level. Modern buildings are fast replacing the old colonial houses with latticed windows, red-tiled roofs and pleasant patios. Wide roads supersede the old narrow streets, but no sooner are they completed than they are already too narrow for the vast volume of traffic.

64 *An impression of the centre of Caracas*

65 *A view of Caracas*

66 *New buildings in Caracas*

Caracas is growing with amazing speed. Bulldozers work night and day to push back the encircling mountains and so enable the city to spread outwards and upwards.

67 *The motor road from Caracas to La Guayra*

A fine trunk road links Caracas to La Guayra, its international airport and harbour.

68 *A welder*

69 *Mining on the Cerro Bolivar*

70 *The construction of a bridge for the Orinoco Mining Company at Puerto Ordaz on the River Orinoco*

South of the River Orinoco the iron-ore of the Guiana Plateau is mined by the Orinoco Mining Company and sent by train to Puerto Ordaz, a newly-constructed harbour at the junction of the Orinoco and the Caroni, where a power-station and smelting-furnace are being built.

71 *Where the floods come yearly in the province of Lara*

Vast areas of the Orinoco basin are covered with impenetrable and partly unexplored jungle. The rolling plains of the 'Llanos', however, are flooded each year in the rainy season and parched in the dry season.

It is interesting to note that a natural waterway, the Casiquiare Canal, links the Orinoco and Amazon river systems. In the course of time this waterway will certainly become economically important.

72 *Powder-dusting the plantations at Valencia*

Realizing that the reserves of oil cannot last for ever, the Venezuelan Government is encouraging the development of agriculture. Research stations and agricultural schools are being built, forests planted and new coffee and cocoa plantations established.

73 *Folk-dancing in the province of Miranda*

74 *Folk-dancing in the province of Lara*

75 *Devil Dance in the province of Miranda*

A curious mixture of Spanish, Indian and African dances is to be found in Venezuela. It is usual for the men alone to dance to the music of a four-stringed guitar, with the rhythmic accompaniment of the 'maracas', a rattle made from a dried gourd. The children dress up for the Devil Dance with evident enjoyment.

76 *The village of Cachopo in the province of Merida*

77 *Primitive threshing on the Sierra de Merida. Horses walk round on the grain until it is separated from the chaff*

The colossal mountain range of the Andes, some 4400 miles long, extends from Southern Chile to Venezuela at its northern end. On its slopes coffee and wheat are cultivated.

Life in the Andes takes little account of national boundaries and its special character can be recognized in Venezuela, Argentina or in Chile.

78 *A young Indian on the Sierra Merida*

Everywhere there is a remarkable sameness about the people, their villages and their customs. The civiliza-tion of the South American Indians was cradled in these mountains, and it was the mountains that drew the first Spanish invaders.

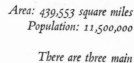

COLOMBIA

Area: 439,553 square miles
Population: 11,500,000

There are three main geographical regions:

1 The Pacific and Caribbean coastal plain
2 The Andean Highlands, running from North to South
3 The Eastern lowlands of the Orinoco and Amazon basins

Exports:
Oil, coffee, cocoa, bananas, platinum and gold

79 *Pamplona, a small town in the Colombian Andes*

Pamplona, the centre of an ancient mining district, lies in the Andes. Founded in 1548, it is one of the many towns in South America which, despite modern developments, manage to retain their colonial character.

80 *The walls of Cartagena*

Cartagena, which lies on the Caribbean coast, has retained its colonial character more than any city in South America, in spite of innumerable attacks by plundering pirates.

There is a story that one day Philip II, peering from the window of his palace in Madrid, complained that he was unable to see the walls of Cartagena which had cost him so much to build. These same walls which took a century to complete, still encircle the 'Heroic City', as Simon Bolivar called it.

81 *Santa Marta*

Santa Marta was also often raided by pirates. This was the first city to be founded in Colombia and from it in 1525, Jimenez de Quesada made his way up the River Magdalena, to conquer the Chibcha Empire. Today Santa Marta is an important port, from which the United Fruit Company exports bananas.

82 *Barranquilla*

Barranquilla, at the mouth of the River Magdalena, is a modern industrial town of over 300,000 in-habitants. It is the most important port in Colombia, and Avianca, the oldest air-line in South America, have an airfield there.

83 *A young girl at Barranquilla*

The women and girls of this region reveal their Spanish origins in their beautiful faces.

84 *A young Negro at Barranquilla*

There are many Negroes in this part of Colombia and their cheerful spirit has left its mark on the local folk music and dancing.

85 *The River Magdalena. Aerial view*

In 1502 the River Magdalena was discovered by Rodrigo de Bastidas. More than 1000 miles long, it has, like most South American rivers which flow through flat country, no well defined main channel. The river bed is much divided and after each rainy season some channels become silted up while others become navigable.

86 *The River Magdalena*

87 *The cook of a river steamer on the River Magdalena*

88 *Passengers in their hammocks, slung between decks, on a river steamer*

89 *Two steamers in the harbour at Berrio on the River Magdalena*

90 *A passenger on his folding bed on a river steamer on the River Magdalena*

91 *Passengers between decks on a river steamer*

Paddle steamers, similar to those formerly to be seen on the Mississippi, navigate the river, propelling strings of laden barges before them. Sandbanks make navigation very difficult and the depth must be sounded throughout the entire journey. Even so, steamers frequently run aground and when this happens a cable is run ashore by row boat and made fast to a tree; the other end is attached to the anchor winch which slowly drags the vessel off the sandbank. Time passes pleasantly on board these steamers, and the ever changing river scenery banishes boredom. There are cabins for the first class passengers, but most of the travellers bring their own bedding or sling hammocks.

92 *A pineapple seller in Barranca Bermeja on the River Magdalena*

93 *Mestizos at Puerto Wilches on the River Magdalena*

94 *A hut near Puerto Wilches*

Often the steamers stop for several hours enabling the passengers to see something of the jungle, and perhaps a group of huts under the banana trees may give a glimpse of the life of the natives.

95 *Bogota, seen from the Tequendama Hotel*

96 *Indians with a jaguar skin on Jimenez de Quesada Street at Bogota*

97 *A street scene in Bogota*

Bogota, the capital of Colombia, is situated about 8000 feet up on the 'Sabana', a green and fertile plateau. Although not far from the Equator, the city has a cool and pleasant climate. Indians from the Andes can often be seen in the city, offering goods for sale, and our photograph shows a father and son from the 'Llanos' who have brought with them a jaguar skin.

98 *Cali, modern skyscrapers in the business quarter*

During the last fifty years Cali has grown into an industrial town of more than 300,000 inhabitants. This rapid development has been favoured by the close proximity of the Pacific port of Buenaventura and by good road and rail communications with other parts of the country.

99 *Coffee bushes under banana trees in the province of Caldas*

100 *Aerial view of the mountains in the province of Caldas*

Colombia is the second largest coffee producer in the world, eighty per cent of the national income being derived from coffee, which is grown at an altitude of between 2000 and 7000 feet on the slopes of the Andes.

ECUADOR

Area: 104,506 square miles
Population: 3,202,750

There are three main geographical regions:

1 The Sierras or Andean Highlands
2 The Pacific coastal plain
3 The Eastern lowlands

Exports: Cocoa, bananas, coffee, balsa wood and Panama hats

COLOUR PLATE II: *Harvesting in the highlands*

101 *Aerial view of the central valleys at Latacunga*

The so-called 'Central Valley', a series of inter-connected valleys, cuts through Ecuador from north to south. Although on or near the Equator, they have a very agreeable climate, being 7000 to 9000 feet above sea-level. All the large towns except Guayaquil lie in these valleys and they support sixty per cent of the people of Ecuador.

102 *The market at Otavalo*

103–5 *Indian women at Otavalo*

The most interesting Indians in South America live in the neighbourhood of Otavalo, where they work in factories or on the big estates to earn enough money to buy back the land taken from them, first by the Incas and later by the Spaniards. The surround-ing country is divided up into small farms, often owned by Indians who are good husbandmen. They are also very skilful weavers and every house has a loom at which the whole family works to produce a cloth of very high quality. These intelligent people soon discovered that it paid them better to buy imported English cloth for their own use and to sell what they made in the cities or in Otavalo market on Saturdays.

They travel during the night from their villages and farms to be on the spot when the market opens at sunrise, each in his allotted place. Here cloth or wool are sold, there pottery and at yet another stall, maize. All this commerce goes on calmly with a remarkable absence of shouting. Salt is a very important com-modity which, since it comes from a distance, is somewhat expensive. Gay glass beads, sold singly or in necklaces, are much coveted as presents by the Otavalo Indian girls.

106 *Façade of the church of La Compañia at Quito*

107 *Interior of the church of La Compañia*

It was in Ecuador that the fate of the Inca Empire was sealed, when Atahualpa, the last of the Incas was murdered by Pizarro in 1533. A year later the city of Quito was founded by Pedro de Alvarado. The most beautiful of the churches surviving from the Colonial period is La Compañia; our picture shows the main façade.

108 *Street scene in Quito*

109 *An Indian woman in a street at Quito*

110 *Indian women with clay pots in front of the church of San Franzisco at Quito*

We are reminded of the fact that Quito was one of the greatest centres of culture in the Spanish Colonial period by the existence in each large town of Ecuador of a House of Culture, where painting, sculpture and music are taught. These institutions are entirely non-political; lectures and concerts are held there and each House has a small printing press which publishes the work of local authors, so that they may be sold cheaply or even distributed free.

111 *Quito in the central valley of Ecuador*

From the nearby mountains there is a magnificent view of Quito lying in its lovely broad valley.

112 *Plaiting Panama hats*

113 *Blocking Panama hats*

114 *The small town of Montecristi*

Panama hats are not made in Panama but at Montecristi, a small village near Guayaquil. These hats, known all over the world, are made of 'toquilla', the local name for bast, and often take several weeks to produce.

115 *Loading bananas at Guayaquil*

116 *Street scene in Guayaquil*

Guayaquil has become the most important port in Ecuador since the Rockefeller Foundation cleared the region of Yellow Fever and Bubonic Plague. But the heat and humidity remain, and the people go about their business in the shade of the arcades which run the whole length of the streets under the houses.

PERU

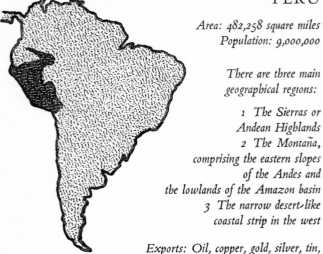

Area: 482,258 square miles
Population: 9,000,000

There are three main
geographical regions:

1 The Sierras or
Andean Highlands
2 The Montaña,
comprising the eastern slopes
of the Andes and
the lowlands of the Amazon basin
3 The narrow desert-like
coastal strip in the west

Exports: Oil, copper, gold, silver, tin,
wolfram, sugar, cotton and wool

COLOUR PLATE I: *The coast near Lima*

117 *In the desert of N. Peru*

Just south of Guayaquil in Ecuador begins the strip of desert that runs along the Pacific coast as far as the middle of Chile. Strange as it may seem, this strip is of the greatest economic importance for Peru.

118 *Oil refinery of the International Petroleum Company at Talara*

119 *Geologists of the International Petroleum Company*

At the northern end of the coastal desert near the border of Ecuador, there is a highly productive oilfield. There is not a single tree in sight and water has to be brought by pipe-line. Peruvians are assisted by North Americans and Britons in operating the oilfield, which is equipped with the most modern machinery. A refinery of the International Petroleum Company at Talara looks curiously out of place set in the middle of the desert.

120 *Collecting guano on one of the islands off the coast of Peru*

121 *Cotton picking on a plantation at Chiclayo*

Where the rivers from the Andes facilitate irrigation, however, the desert ends abruptly and we enter a green and fertile region in which sugar, cotton and rice grow abundantly.

From the islands off the coast thousands of tons of guano are gathered each year.

122 *Young fisherman in a reed boat*

For centuries the Peruvian boys have gone 'riding' out to fish in their reed boats which they call 'little sea-horses'.

123 *The archbishop's palace at Lima*

124 *A balcony of the colonial period at the Torre Tagle palace at Lima*

In 1535 Francisco Pizarro founded Lima, the City of the Kings, which for 300 years was the seat of the Viceroy and the most important city of the Spanish Colonial Empire. No other South American capital has so preserved its ancient character. In the Inner City there is hardly a house without a balcony. The finest of these old buildings are the Torre Tagle palace and the archbishop's palace.

125 *A modern residential quarter for employees in the vicinity of Lima*

126 *The Stadium at Lima*

With over a million inhabitants, Lima is the fifth largest city in South America. New workers' houses have been built in some parts of the city and every Sunday thousands of sports lovers pour into the huge stadium.

127 *The railway near Oroya*

Indians and Mestizos have got quite used to the railway which climbs from Lima 15,800 feet into the Andes, thereby linking the capital with the mining and smelting centre of Oroya.

128 *A herd of llamas at Cuzco*

On the roads of the Peruvian and Bolivian Andes one encounters groups of Indians driving herds of llamas. Their possessions they carry on their backs tied in a cloth and they wander all day in the wake of their animals. Llamas, huanacos and alpacas, all of the camel tribe, live high on the mountains where farming is impossible, and are almost the sole support of the Indians, who eat their flesh, drink their milk, and collect their dung which they can barter for other necessities. From the wool they weave cloth on primitive looms for their own clothes or to sell. The llama is also very valuable as a beast of burden.

129 *An Indian at Hatuntaqui*

The Andes cover one third of the territory of Peru and most of the people who live there are Indians, who struggle to make a poor living on the lonely heights and in the valleys. Farming is possible only in very protected places and then only below a certain height, and these needy people are to be admired for the way they seek to grow crops on tiny plots of land with only the smallest hope of success. Very few Indians own any land; they live in small communities and must work a few days a month for the landowner or tend his herds. For this they are paid a very small wage and given salt, spirits or coca without which they cannot live. Coca is the dried leaves of *Erythroxylon coca*, a native plant of Peru and Bolivia. The Indians chew the coca leaves and it appears to help them to endure the high altitudes.

130 *A street in Cuzco*

Strolling through the streets of Cuzco the traveller encounters the past at every step. Cuzco has been called the Athens of South America on account of the ruins of the beautiful Inca buildings which may still be seen, both in the city and in the surrounding countryside. Cuzco was partly destroyed by the earthquake of 1950, but the ancient walls which survived the attacks of the Spanish invaders still stand.

131 *The lowlands of the Amazon basin in the department of Loreto*

132 *A jungle river in the Amazon basin in the department of Loreto*

133 *Pile-dwellings near Iquitos, on the Amazon, at high tide*

More than half of Peruvian territory lies in the Amazon basin and from the eastern slopes of the Andes to the borders of Brazil and Colombia the country is covered by impenetrable tropical forest. Here the Ucayali and Marañon rivers unite to become the River Amazon. This vast region has an enormous wealth of natural resources as yet quite untapped. The only settlements are on the Amazon and its tributaries and the largest of these, Iquitos, is 1200 miles by air from the capital. The products of this region must travel 7000 miles round the north of the continent before they can reach Callao, the port of Lima. In the rainy season the Amazon often rises as much as 30 feet, flooding huge tracts of land.

134 *The sandstone porch of the church of Santa Cruz at Juli*

135 *The dome of the church at Pomata*

136 *The church of San Pedro at Juli*

Many churches in Peru and Bolivia, like the one at Juli which one of our pictures shows, display a curious mixture of architectural styles all dating from different periods. An Indian influence can be recognized in the decoration which gives a special character to the South American Late Baroque of this region. The choir of this church is painted with Indian patterns; it also shows the influence of the Potosi school and is topped by a Gothic cupola. The stone carvings on the dome of the church at Pomata, on Lake Titicaca, are the finest example of the enduring influence of the Indians.

137 *The Altiplano—the highland between Bolivia and Peru*

In South Peru the Andes massif divides, and one arm, the Cordillera Real, curves in a great arc to the east to reunite in North Argentina and Chile with the Cordillera Maritima, which follows the coastline. Between these Cordilleras lies the 'Altiplano' or 'Puna', a plateau with an average height of about 13,000 feet. Small, half-derelict villages, set far apart, seem lost in the unending landscape.

138 *The church at Llika in the Bolivian Highlands*

139 *Musicians with pan-pipes and drums on the square at Juli*

140 *Folk-dancing on the square at Juli*

Seeing a group of Indians dancing in the village square, one may well ask where in these lonely parts they all come from, and having come, what should make them dance. Some may have come to make a vow at the church, others to consult their lawyer concerning the boundaries of their land. And now, their business done, they meet their friends to drink and dance for an hour, for an entire day or for as much as a week, for as long as their money lasts or until the musicians are weary of blowing their flutes and banging their drums—or more probably until they are all too tipsy to go on any longer.

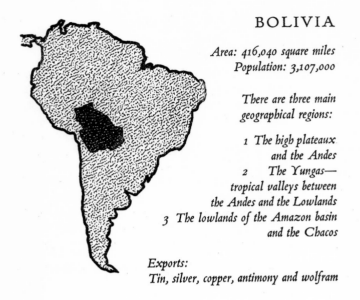

BOLIVIA

Area: 416,040 square miles
Population: 3,107,000

*There are three main
geographical regions:*

*1 The high plateaux
and the Andes*
*2 The Yungas—
tropical valleys between
the Andes and the Lowlands*
*3 The lowlands of the Amazon basin
and the Chacos*

Exports:
Tin, silver, copper, antimony and wolfram

COLOUR PLATE III: *Devil Mask at Copacabana*

141–2 *The wolfram mine, 'Bolsa Negra', at the foot of the Illimani in Bolivia*

Mining was in progress throughout the Andes region long before the arrival of the Spaniards and is still of great importance in the economy of Peru and Bolivia. Tin, lead, gold, silver and wolfram are mined at different levels and the altitude of some of the mines is so great that very few Europeans are able to work there. Our pictures were taken at the wolfram mine called 'Bolsa Negra' (the Black Sack), in Bolivia. In the background rises Illimani, one of the highest peaks in the Andes (21,300 feet).

143 *Landscape at Lake Titicaca*

Lake Titicaca lies 12,500 feet up, in a plateau between the two arms of the Andes; it takes its name from the Island of Titicaca. An Indian legend tells how Viracocha, the Creator, raised the sun and moon into the heavens from this island, and there is also a tradition that Manco Capac, the first of the Incas, was born here. This region of South America is one of the most beautiful in the world and is the most densely populated part of the high plateaux of Bolivia and Peru. Long before the arrival of the Spaniards there were small settlements here, and one of these, Copacabana, has quite a history.

144 *The Mountain of Calvary at the Holy Place of Copacabana*

Copacabana was an Indian meeting-place, to which people from all parts of 'Tahuantinsuyo', the Inca Empire, flocked each year to take part in a festival held on the Island of the Sun. The Spaniards, passing through on their march to the south, noticed that some of the Indian ceremonies and customs resembled their own, and built a small chapel. In the course of time Copacabana became a famous place of pilgrimage, and a great festival in honour of the Virgin was held each year. The festival centred about a statue of the Virgin, carved by Indian craftsmen. Even today the ancient traditions of the Indians are not completely obscured and may be observed in the Catholic liturgy in the temple, in the religious procession and in the ceremonial dances held in the great square. The Indians see nothing strange in going straight from the native fortune-tellers to the Confessional, and when they follow the Way of the Cross, murmuring a prayer at each station, they do not forget an offering for 'Pacha Mama', Mother Earth, which they lay at the foot of the Cross.

For the festival the Indians deck themselves in grotesque costumes and masks. Some of these masks resemble Chinese dragons or the curious mask-like patterns with which pre-Colombian pottery is ornamented; others stem from their own lively imaginations.

145 *La Paz, the capital of Bolivia*

146 *'La Chola', a mestizo woman*

La Paz lies at a greater altitude than any other large city in the world; its 350,000 people live 12,000 feet above sea-level, where the rarefied atmosphere renders movement difficult. Eighty-five per cent of the people of Bolivia are Indians and Mestizos, and the life of the city is dominated by them.

147 *Part of the façade of a colonial house at Potosi*

148 *Potosi*

The Spaniards soon discovered that Bolivia had a wealth of silver and began to search for silver ore. In 1545 they discovered the famous 'Cerro Rico', the Silver Mountain, and founded the town of Potosi at the foot of it. Twenty thousand million silver coins were struck there and sent home to Spain. The huge mint with wooden machines still stands in the centre of the town. At one time the population rose to 160,000, but when the silver ceased to flow from the mines Potosi became a sleepy and lifeless town. Of late, however, modern machines have begun to burrow into the mountain to bring up tin from its depths, and the city is awakening to new life.

149 *Aerial view of Cochabamba*

Cochabamba, 8300 feet above sea-level, is the second largest town in Bolivia. Owing to the delightful climate it has become a holiday resort for the Bolivians.

150 *An Indian in front of a colonial church in Cochabamba*

Little has changed in the Indians' way of life; illiterate, unassuming, accustomed to service, he bears his burden without complaint.

151 *A street corner in Cochabamba*

A 'Chola' or Mestizo woman, in her typical white cardboard hat, sits yawning at a street corner.

152 *An Indian at Tarabuco*

153 *Indian women at Tarabuco*

The Bolivian Government is at present engaged in a very interesting experiment. Tracts of unused land have been expropriated from the great landowners and divided among Indians. They are given instruction in farming, and an attempt is being made to interest them in the cultivation of valuable crops, in the hope that they may become useful members of the community. They have been enfranchised and now attend political meetings. They wear badges, which they cannot read, and listen attentively to speeches which they cannot understand. In time these Indians, so long ignored and neglected, may perhaps shed their apathy.

154 *A street in Santa Cruz*

155 *Santa Cruz*

Seventy per cent of Bolivian territory lies in the lowlands of the rivers Amazon and La Plata. Whilst air transport has done something to improve conditions in the north, it is the south that will now see the most rapid progress. The Santa Cruz region is now linked to Cochabamba by road, and to Brazil by rail

ARGENTINA

Area: 1,073,700 square miles
Population: 18,500,000

There are four main geographical regions:

1 The Andean Highlands
2 The lowlands of the Chaco and the land between the rivers Parana and Uruguay
3 The Pampas
4 The lowlands and the Patagonian plateau

Exports: Meat, grain, hides, wool, vegetable oil, fruit, milk products and tannin

COLOUR PLATE IV: *The Iguazu Falls, Argentina and Brazil*

156 *Quebrada del Obispo—the Valley of the Bishop near Salta*

157 *A street in Santa Victoria*

Argentina was ruled by the Viceroy of Peru for two and a half centuries from the time the first colonizers crossed the Andean plateau.

The passage of time has left the little villages hidden in the valleys of northern Argentina quite unchanged. Today still mules and horses are the only means of getting to market.

Life is easier for the owners of the large estancias. For the most part they live in the towns and leave their estates to be managed by others. Most of these estates are not suitable for farming owing to a shortage of water; one acre of the bare hillside will scarcely support a single sheep.

158 *Wine jars in the Calchaqui valley near Salta*

In a few places vines can be cultivated, and here and there in the cellars the old earthenware wine jars are still used.

159 *Before a house in the Calchaqui valley*

Nights are cool in the mountains and the sunshine of early morning is very welcome.

160 *A woman spinning at Santiago del Estero*

In the province of Santiago del Estero the women still spin yarn for their looms.

161 *In front of the Rancho—the foreman's hut—on the Pampa*

162 *A Gaucho*

Scattered groups of trees, a wire fence running straight to the horizon, a birds' nest on a wooden gate-post, the silhouette of a rider and his dog slowly wending their way beneath the dome of the pale blue sky—that is the Argentina of the limitless plains.

This region, now one of the richest in Argentina, was useless for cattle raising until wire fences were used to divide up the rolling Pampas. The value of the land has changed but not the character of the men who live on it. It is this special character that has made the 'Gauchos' something more than mere cattle-men. The word 'Gaucho' implies not only skill and courage, but also generosity, hospitality and kindness. The phrase "He is a true Gaucho", is often applied to a man who has never mounted a horse, and when it is said of a foreigner it is a very great honour.

Plate 161 shows some men of the Pampas. On the left sits the 'Estanciero', the owner of one of the oldest estancias in Argentina. He has been showing his herd to a cattle buyer and now rests before the 'Rancho', his foreman's cabin. Naturally the seat in the centre will be offered to the guest. The foreman had seen them coming from afar and has put meat to roast over the glowing charcoal, so that he may offer an 'Asado' to his guests. While the meal slowly cooks they sit peacefully drinking 'Mate', a kind of tea made from the dried leaves of a shrub, served in a small gourd and imbibed through a silver tube.

163 *A cattle-show at Buenos Aires*

The agricultural show held in the capital is a great occasion for the Argentine cattle-breeders and farmers, and thousands come to watch the parade of the prize-winning animals.

164 *A Tropilla, or team of horses*

Nothing can supplant the horse in the life of the country people. A well-trained team of horses is the pride of every 'Estanciero'.

165 *The Avenida Presidente R. Saenz Peña in Buenos Aires*

166 *Entrance to a business house in Buenos Aires*

Ullrich Schmidel, a German mercenary, describes in his book, *Reise nach Spanien und Indien,* the first unhappy efforts to found the city of Buenos Aires. In 1533 Don Pedro de Mendoza was unable to defend the little colony against the Indians and it was not until 1580 that a second attempt was made, this time successfully, to found the city which, in the course of time, became the most important of all South American capitals.

167 *The Beagle Canal in Tierra del Fuego*

168 *The shore of the Rio Gallegos*

In the extreme south, no less than 2300 miles from the most northerly town in Argentina, the Beagle Canal cuts through Tierra del Fuego. On the Rio Gallegos in Patagonia the difference between high and low water is so great that in order to land, ships sail as near the shore as possible and wait there until the ebb tide leaves them high and dry.

169 *A rider in Patagonia*

It is possible to ride on through the windswept Patagonian steppe for hours or even days on end. It is usual to have at least two horses, one of which trots behind with the provisions until the roles are reversed.

Thousands of sheep are bred in Patagonia and the amount of wool exported is considerable.

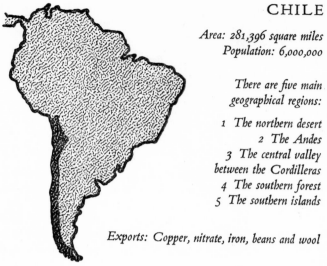

CHILE

Area: 281,396 square miles
Population: 6,000,000

There are five main geographical regions:

1 The northern desert
2 The Andes
3 The central valley between the Cordilleras
4 The southern forest
5 The southern islands

Exports: Copper, nitrate, iron, beans and wool

170 *Aerial view of the coast of S. Chile*

Benjamin Supercaseaux called Chile 'The country of crazy geography.' It is a strip of land 2800 miles long, 200 miles wide at its broadest point and 50 miles at its narrowest, bordering the Pacific from Cape Horn to the Peruvian frontier. In the south, the icy currents and stormy seas of the far from Pacific Ocean labour diligently to break up the coastline. Thousands of islands have been created and behind them the sea eats deep into the land, as it does in the Norwegian fiords. The mainland is covered with dense, humid jungle which rarely sees the sun.

171 *Puerto Montt*

Puerto Montt is an important harbour for the island people, to which they come to buy provisions and post their letters. For this is the terminus of Chile's trunk railway, 1500 miles long.

172 *The coast at Arica*

173 *A view of part of Arica*

The free port of Arica lies at the other end of the country on the edge of the northern desert. Bolivia, which is linked to Chile by rail, has free access to it.

174 *A view of part of Santiago, taken from the hill of Santa Lucia. In the foreground, the Catholic University*

Santiago, the capital of Chile, was founded in 1541 by Pedro de Valdivia. It lies in a fertile plain at the foot of a hill called Santa Lucia, from which there is a fine view of this beautiful city. The Cordillera rises abruptly only sixty miles away, and on clear days its range of snow-capped peaks rising to 20,000 feet can be seen. The proximity of the Andes has its disadvantages: often in bad weather the planes of the international airlines are unable to land in Santiago.

175 *Valparaiso*

176 *A suburb of Valparaiso*

Valparaiso is the most important port, not only of Chile but on the whole Pacific coast. The city occupies the slopes of mountains which encircle the bay in a wide arc. To make life easier for the people countless lifts have been built, and for a few cents they can ride to the upper quarter of the city.

177–8 *The Sewell copper mine of the Braden Copper Co.*

Chile is the second largest producer of copper in the world. The Sewell copper mine of the Braden Copper Company, with its bold position on the steep slopes of the Andes, is reminiscent of the Inca city, Machu Picchu.

179 *Aconcagua, from the air*

Aconcagua (23,000 feet) is the highest mountain in the Andes.

PARAGUAY

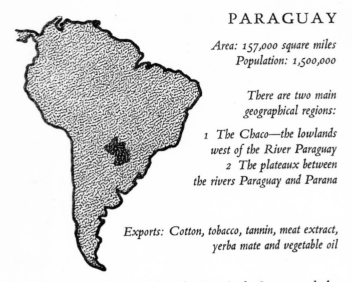

Area: 157,000 square miles
Population: 1,500,000

There are two main
geographical regions:

1 The Chaco—the lowlands
west of the River Paraguay
2 The plateaux between
the rivers Paraguay and Parana

Exports: Cotton, tobacco, tannin, meat extract,
yerba mate and vegetable oil

It was in 1537 that the Spaniards first crossed the La Plata, and afterwards the Paraguay, in their search for a route to the riches of the Andes. They had several clashes with the Indians and finally, on Ascension Day, they conquered Chief Lambaré and succeeded in occupying a sheltered bay of the river. They called the place 'Asuncion', now the capital of Paraguay. The city is widely dispersed on hilly ground and is gay with orange trees and tropical flowers. Early each morning there is a cheerful clip-clop of hooves, as the fruit-selling women ride through the streets on their little donkeys.

180 *Monkey-Puzzle trees on the borders of Paraguay and Brazil*

The Monkey-Puzzle (*Araucaria brasiliensis*), the tallest South American tree, can be seen growing near the Brazilian border.

181 *A woman of Paraguay making lace*

The famous lace made by the women of Paraguay is called 'ñanduty', which means 'cobweb'.

182–6 *Toba Indians*

187 *Chulupi Indian*

The people of Paraguay are for the most part Mestizos whose ancestors were Guarani Indians, one of the most advanced races of the lowlands. They were farmers and, being a friendly people, they accepted without opposition the occupation of their land by the Jesuits. Even today this is the dominant race in Paraguay. The people have retained their own language, Guarani, which is on an equal footing with Spanish. Our photographs show various types of Indians from the Chaco.

URUGUAY

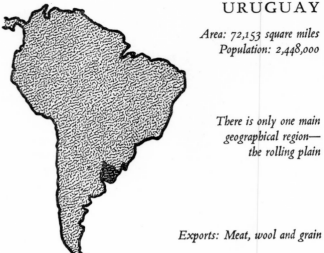

Area: 72,153 square miles
Population: 2,448,000

There is only one main
geographical region—
the rolling plain

Exports: Meat, wool and grain

Uruguay, the smallest of the South American countries has been fortunate in having had a very wise President, José Battle y Ordoñez, whose guiding principle was that if the rich are a little less rich, the poor will be a little less poor. The succeeding government followed the same principle, and Uruguay is now the most advanced State in South America. A type of State Socialism has been introduced under which the State controls all commercial and industrial undertakings by means of non-political institutions, especially created for the purpose.

188 *A cattle-breeder on the Pampa*

189–90 *The beach at Carrasco near Montevideo*

191 *A gaming-table at Punta del Este*

192 *In front of a club at Punta del Este*

193 *Brazilian holiday-makers at Punta del Este*

Cattle-breeding and agriculture are certainly still basic factors in the economy of Uruguay, but the tourist trade plays quite as important a role. The cool climate, beautiful beaches, good hotels, and not least the Casinos, attract many holiday-makers from the neighbouring countries.

BRAZIL

Area: 3,228,045 square miles
Population: 56,000,000

There are four main geographical regions:

1 The Guiana plateau
2 The lowlands of the Amazon basin
3 The central and southern plateaux
4 The Parana plateau

Exports: Coffee, cocoa, tobacco, cotton, wood, fruit and iron ore

COLOUR PLATE V: *Dockers playing dominoes at Santos*

194 *Copacabana, the famous beach at Rio de Janeiro seen from Corcovado*

195 *Santa Teresa, a district of Rio de Janeiro*

The much vaunted beauty of Rio de Janeiro is enhanced by the mountains which rise steeply from the sea, but few realize how these same mountains hinder the expansion of this city with its two-and-a-half million inhabitants. It is forced to follow the capricious twists of the Atlantic coast and the beautiful Bay of Guanbara, clinging to the land between the sea and the mountains, creeping into the valleys and up their sloping sides. Tunnels have been bored through the mountains to make communication between separate districts of the city possible.

196 *Huts and skyscrapers*

197 *The Aqueduct, now a tramway bridge in the centre of Rio de Janeiro*

198 *Street life in the Avenida Rio Branco*

Rio de Janeiro is a city of great contrasts, but far from offending, these contrasts add to its attraction. A tiny cottage beside a block of offices, a moorish-style house beside a modern skyscraper, blend charmingly under the tropical sky. The old aqueduct in the city centre is no encumbrance; the tramways now run over and under it, and one block away the business life of the city is in full swing.

199 *Street scene on the Avenida Nilo Peçanha in Rio de Janeiro*

The Portuguese style of many of the old streets and churches give Rio a distinctive appearance, unlike the cities of the Spanish half of the continent. The charming open-air cafés, which are to be found everywhere, help one to endure the extreme heat.

200 *The Ministry of Education, Rio de Janeiro*

The happy and carefree temperament of the Brazilians has produced a bold and unfettered architectural style. It is not so long since Le Corbusier was called in to prepare plans for the Brazilian Ministry of Education, which is illustrated here, and now Brazilian architects and artists have collaborated in the United Nations building in New York. The influence of Brazilian architecture can be seen all over South America.

201 *This girl has a German father and a Brazilian mother*

202 *A Customs Officer in Rio de Janeiro*

203 *News-vendor in São Paulo*

204 *There is no colour bar in Brazil*

There is no colour bar in Brazil; the daughter of a German and a Brazilian woman feels in no way superior to the mulatto who serves her in a shop and the negro newsvendor does not suffer from an inferiority complex.

205 *São Paulo*

206 *Mosaics on the offices of 'O Estado' by the Brazilian artist, Di Cavalcanti*

207 *The offices of the newspaper 'O Estado' at São Paulo*

Since the beginning of the century São Paulo has become a metropolis with a population of over three million. It is the economic and cultural centre of Brazil and is on the way to becoming the most important city in South America.

Artists from all over the world send their work to the Biennial Exhibition of Modern Art, held in São Paulo. Mosaics by Brazilian artists can be seen on many of the modern houses in the city.

Brazil is the largest coffee-producing country in the world. Each year millions of bags of coffee are exported from Santos.

208 *A coffee taster at Santos*

There is no substitute for a coffee taster. He has to smell and taste the raw and roasted coffee, and the most fragrant and best flavoured are then sorted into various grades.

209 *Loading coffee at Santos*

210 *Part of the harbour at Santos*

211 *Aerial view of Bello Horizonte*

212 *A skyscraper at Bello Horizonte*

Like many South American towns, Bello Horizonte, the capital of the province of Minas Gerães, grew erratically, and is still in process of development.

Two hundred and fifty years ago gold was discovered there and men flocked from all parts of Brazil in the hope of getting rich quickly. When the gold ran out after less than a century the region lapsed into obscurity, and only came to life again with the discovery and exploitation of the iron ore deposits.

Now Bello Horizonte, with 300,000 inhabitants, is rapidly becoming a most important industrial centre.

213 *A view of the atrium of the church at Congonhas do Campo, showing one of Antonio Lisboa's statues.*

214 *Some of Lisboa's Statues of prophets*

These remarkable statues of twelve prophets were carved by a mulatto, Antonio Franzisco Lisboa in the late eighteenth century, and stand in front of the old church in the little village of Congonhas do Campo.

215 *A village street at Congonhas do Campo*

In several towns of the province of Minas Gerães most beautiful houses and churches built in the Brazilian Baroque style are still to be seen.

216 *In the interior of Espirito Santo*

217 *A hut under coco-palms in the province of Espirito Santo*

The landscape of Brazil offers great variety, which is reflected in the life of the people. Where nature provides coconuts, bananas and breadfruit, a hut under the palm trees is all that is needed for a pleasant, easy existence; but in the valleys of the high plateau life is very different, and the people must work hard to make a living. A century ago a group of immigrants from southern Germany settled in the province of Espirito Santo, imposing their national character on the region. Their houses are built in the style of their forefathers and their customs have changed little—but it is rare to come across a single one who any longer speaks German.

218 *Victoria*

Victoria, the capital of Espirito Santo, is the port used for shipping iron ore from Minas Gerães.

219 *The sacristy of the church of San Franzisco at Bahia*

220 *The head of a figure of Christ by the artist Chagas el Mestizo*

221 *A street in the ancient city of San Salvador de Bahia*

The picturesque old town of San Salvador de Bahia is a source of delight to the visitor who wanders among its rambling streets. Baroque palaces and churches remind us that it was once one of the richest towns in South America and the capital of Brazil. Bahia is still the dream city of every Brazilian, although its colonial character is gradually disappearing. The less sentimental visitor from overseas associates it with the export of tobacco and cocoa.

Of the 365 churches which Bahia boasts, the most beautiful is the church of the monastery of St Francis of Assisi. The statue of Christ was carved at the end of the seventeenth century by 'Chagas el Mestizo'.

222 *A gambler, San Salvador de Bahia*

The appearance of this owner of an illegal gambling house may not inspire confidence, but he can be relied upon to pay his debts.

223 *A Negro, San Salvador de Bahia*

224 *Aerial view of the city of Manaos*

225 *The Opera House at Manaos*

One thousand miles upstream in the middle of the Amazon region lies Manaos. During the rubber boom this city rocketed to fantastic heights of luxury. There are still people who remember that Caruso once sang in the short-lived Opera House there, whose doors are now permanently closed. Manaos has lost its importance since the East Indies broke into the rubber market. In view of the enormous potentialities of the region, however, this city with its fine situation at the junction of the Rio Negro with the Amazon may yet enjoy an era of renewed prosperity.

226 *Sailing boats on the Amazon*

227 *A fish vendor at Santarem*

Travelling by air over the Santarem region one can see below the dark waters of the Tapajoz and the yellowish waters of the Amazon running side by side. In the rainy season the river becomes a huge sea whose limits are not visible even from the air.

228 *A vaqueiro, or cowboy, at Santa Ana in N.E. Brazil*

THE GUIANAS

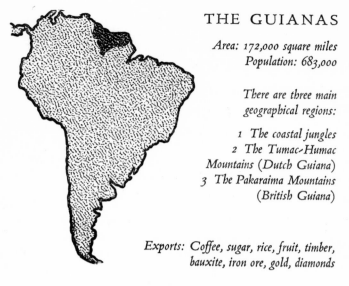

Area: 172,000 square miles
Population: 683,000

*There are three main
geographical regions:*

*1 The coastal jungles
2 The Tumac-Humac
Mountains (Dutch Guiana)
3 The Pakaraima Mountains
(British Guiana)*

*Exports: Coffee, sugar, rice, fruit, timber,
bauxite, iron ore, gold, diamonds*

In a book which appeared in London in 1596 Sir Walter Raleigh wrote of his travels in the Amazon and Orinoco basins and described a rich and beautiful country he had visited. English, French and Dutch hastened to colonize the region but what they found did not by any means correspond with Raleigh's enthusiastic account. The three Guianas lie in the hottest and most humid part of the continent and life in such a climate is anything but pleasant.

229 *A plantation in French Guiana*

230 *Rapids on a tributary of the River Orinoco*

Dense, steamy jungle covers most of the country and there are few large settlements except on the coast. Here and there where the jungle has been cleared, the soil has proved favourable to tropical farming.

The rivers of the Guianas are too fast-flowing to be navigable, and the population of the interior is so sparse that it is uneconomic to build roads or railways. Such important towns as there are lie at the mouths of the rivers and only a fraction of the total area is inhabited.

231 *Cayenne*

232 *The main street of Cayenne*

233 *Cayenne—fruit-sellers*

234 *The hospital at Cayenne*

Cayenne, capital of French Guiana, never a wealthy or important city, is now, owing to the closing of the prison colony on Devil's Island, silent and moribund. Only in the early morning when the fishermen and small farmers cry their wares, or after sunset, does the city come to life.

A modern hospital and leper colony are in great contrast to their dilapidated surroundings.

235 *A hair-dresser in Paramaribo, Dutch Guiana*

236 *A Hindu festival at Paramaribo*

Less than ten per cent of the people of the Guianas are European, and nowhere is there a greater mixture of races. An Arab barber cuts a Negro's hair; in their homes the Indians celebrate according to their ancient customs. Many Indonesians have been brought in to swell the population.

237 *Street scene in Paramaribo*

In Surinam, Dutch Guiana, the colonization is partly on Dutch and partly on English lines.

238 *Workers' families at Georgetown, British Guiana*

239 *A bank in Georgetown*

240 *Workers' houses at Georgetown*

Georgetown, the capital of British Guiana, is very different from Paramaribo, a town of comparable size. It is much more spacious; the houses are set well apart and the roads are wider. Business premises and dwelling-houses were nearly all made of wood until after the fire of 1945, when concrete began to be used.

Verandas are essential for domestic life in the heat of the Guianas and no house, however poor, is without one.

241 *A Negro woman*

No matter how hot and humid it may be, with a topee, the minimum of clothes and a smile, one can put up with anything.

The author wishes to express his gratitude to the following: Professor A. Grondona, for advice on historical and geographical questions; Reginald Debenham Clark for helping to plan the book, and Ricardo de Angelis for editorial assistance. In particular the author wishes to mention Mr Domingo Bezzola, Director of the Grillon Hotel, Lima, Peru, and Messrs Franke and Heidecke (Rolleiflex) of Brunswick, Germany, without whose help this book could not have been produced.

Finally the author would like to thank the following organizations for valuable help with photographs: Esso Standard, Brazil and Argentina; Creole Petroleum Corporation, Venezuela; Ministerio Educación Nacional, Venezuela; International Petroleum Company, Colombia; Shell, Colombia y Ecuador.

PICTURE CREDITS

THE PLATES

Venezuela

56

57

61

62   *Venezuel*

Venezuela

67

Venezuela

68/69

Venezuela

73

74

75

Venezue

Venezuela

Colomb

82

Colombia

83

Colombi

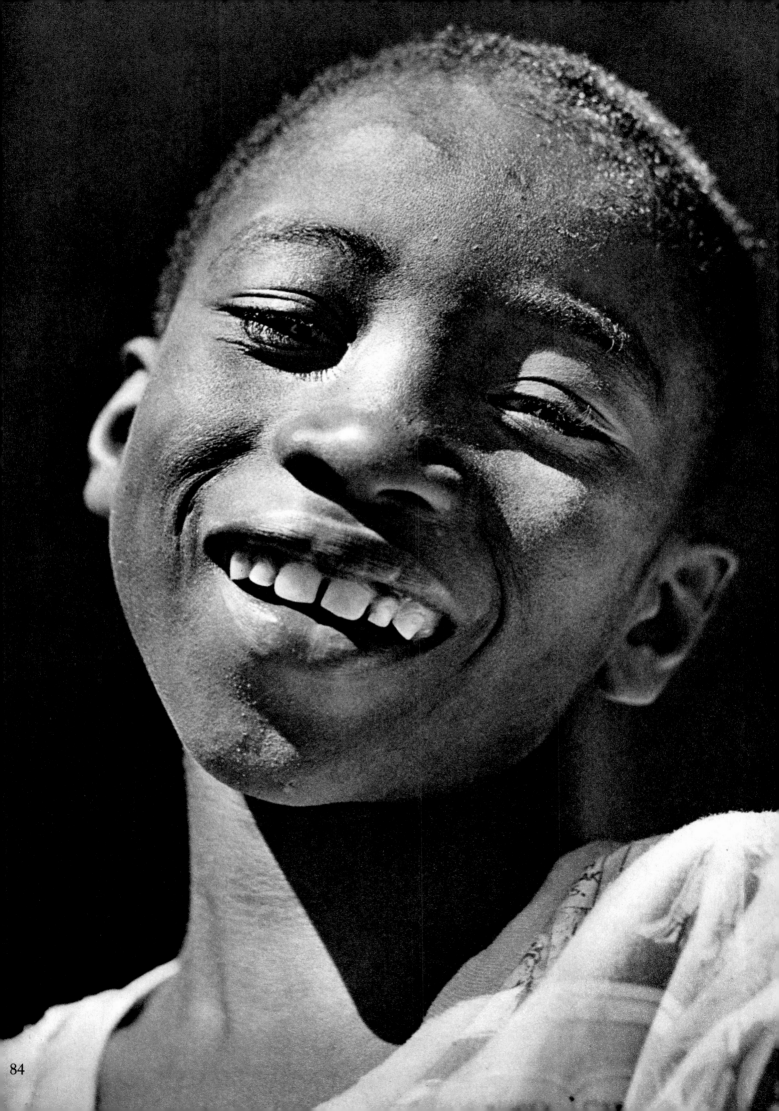

85

Colombia

86

87/88

Colombia

Colombia

96

97

98

Colomb

Ecuador

103

104

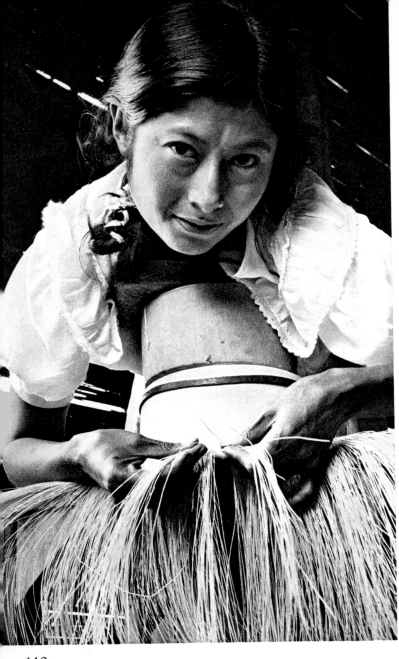

112

113

114

Ecuador

Ecuador

117

Per

118

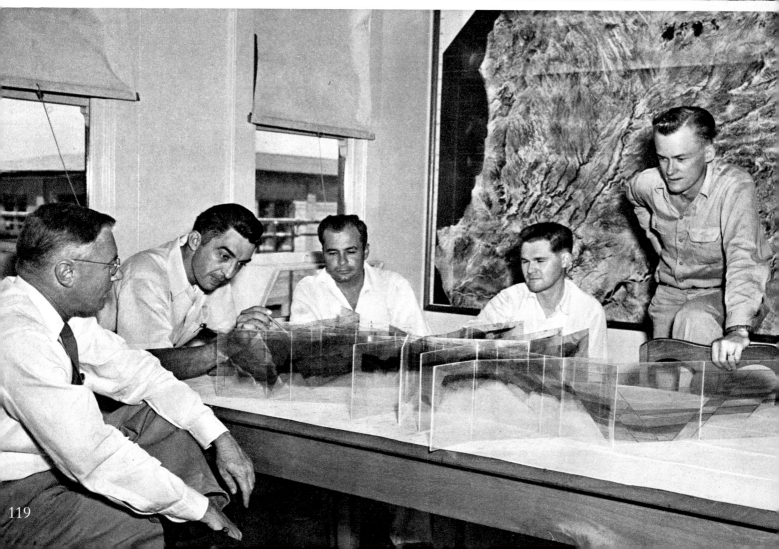

119

120

121

Pe

Peru

123

124

25

26

127

129

Per

131

132

Peru

134

135

136

137

138

139

140

Boli

143

4

Bolivia

Bolivia

147

148

49

Bolivia

Bolivia

153

Bolivia

Bolivi

156

Argentin

Argentina

1

Argentina

162

163

Argentina

165

167

168

Argentina

Chi.

1

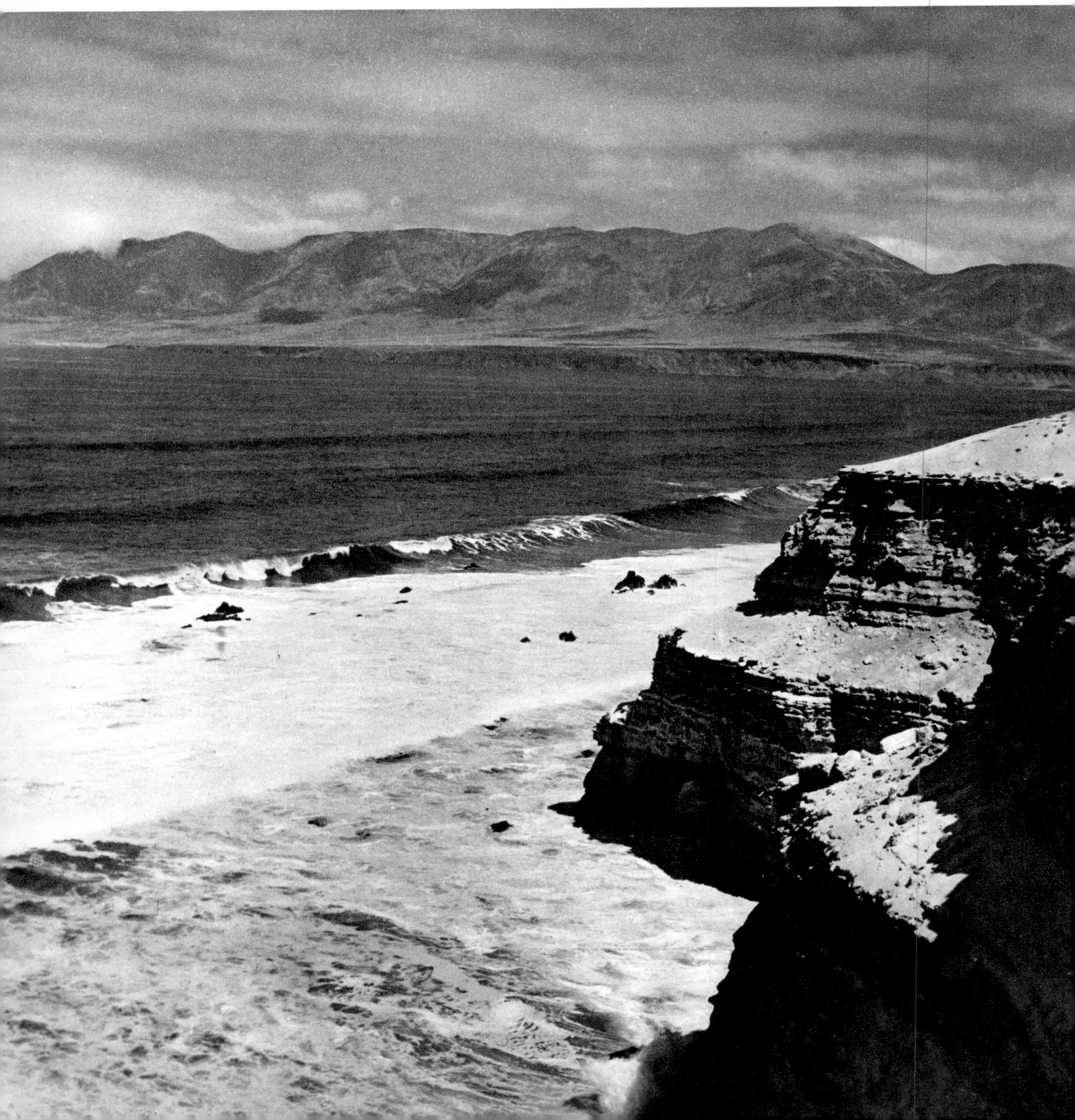

73

Chile

174

175

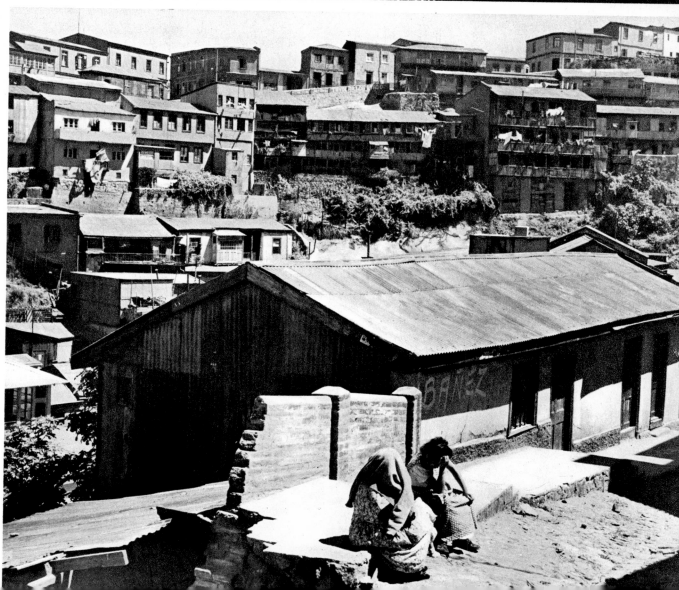

176

177

178

Chile

1

Paraguay

182

183/4

186/7 *Paraguay*

188

189/190

Uruguay

194

Braz

196

197

198

199

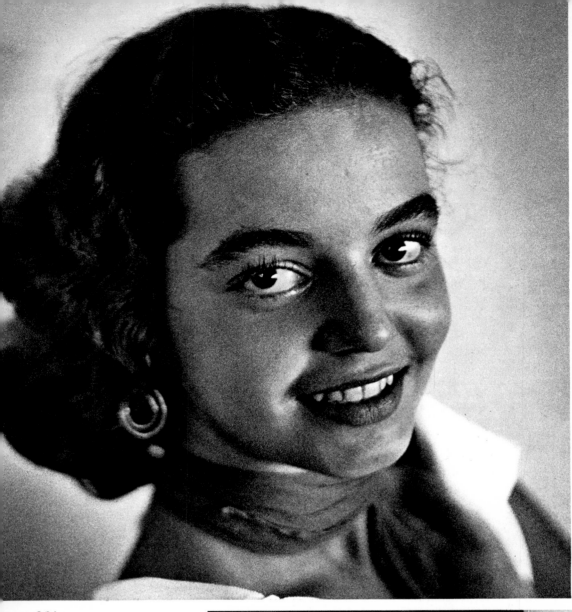

201

202

203

204

205

206

209

Brazil 210

211

Braz

215

Brazil

216

217

218

219

220

Brazil

222

Brazi

225

226

Braz.

228

229

230

231

Las
Guayanas

232

233

234

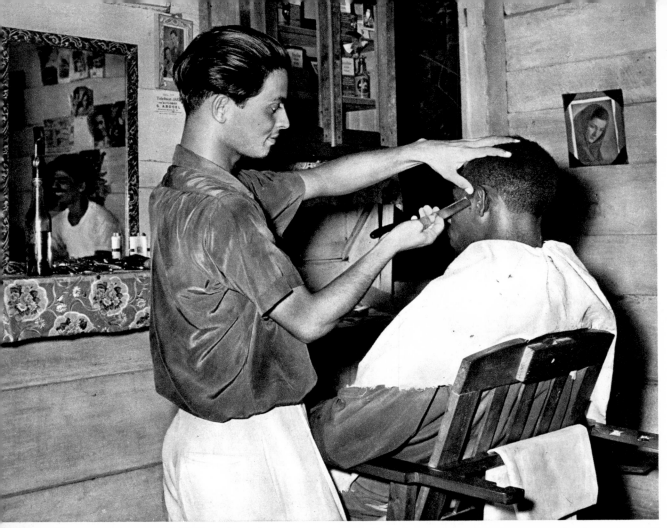

Las Guayanas

238

239

240

Las Guayanas